RECIPES

Publications International, Ltd.

TABLE OF CONTENTS

STARTERS & SOUPS

SPICY BBQ PARTY FRANKS
MAKES 6 TO 8 SERVINGS

1 tablespoon butter

1 package (1 pound) cocktail franks

⅓ cup *Coca-Cola*®

⅓ cup ketchup

2 tablespoons hot pepper sauce

1 tablespoon cider vinegar

2 tablespoons packed dark brown sugar

Heat butter in medium skillet over medium heat. Pierce cocktail franks with fork. Add franks to skillet and brown slightly.

Pour in *Coca-Cola*, ketchup, hot pepper sauce and vinegar. Stir in brown sugar; reduce heat.

Cook until sticky glaze is achieved. Serve with toothpicks.

TWIN CHEESE DIP

MAKES ABOUT 3 CUPS

About ¾ pound (12 ounces) sharp Cheddar cheese

1 package (4 ounces) Roquefort cheese

1 clove garlic

¾ cup *Coca-Cola*®, divided

2 tablespoons soft margarine

1 tablespoon grated onion

1½ teaspoons Worcestershire sauce

1 teaspoon dry mustard

¼ teaspoon salt

⅛ teaspoon hot pepper sauce

Grate Cheddar cheese into large mixing bowl. Add crumbled Roquefort. Put garlic through press; add to cheeses with ½ cup *Coca-Cola* and remaining ingredients.

Place mixture in food processor; pulse until combined. Gradually add remaining *Coca-Cola*, then process until mixture is fairly smooth, light and fluffy. Pack into covered container. Chill. Best if refrigerated overnight.

TIP

This dip keeps very well for a week or more. Twin Cheese Dip is good with raw vegetables, as a spread for cocktail breads or crackers or even as a sandwich filling.

STARTERS & SOUPS

COCA-COLA® CHILI

MAKES 4 TO 6 SERVINGS

1 pound ground beef

1 medium onion, chopped

4 stalks celery, chopped

1 can (about 15 ounces) tomato sauce

1 can (14½ ounces) beef broth

2 tablespoons chili powder

1 teaspoon garlic powder

1 teaspoon paprika

1 teaspoon ground cumin

1 can (15 ounces) kidney beans, drained

1 cup *Coca-Cola®*

1 teaspoon hot pepper sauce

Salt and black pepper

Spray 3-quart Dutch oven with nonstick cooking spray. Cook beef, onion and celery over medium-high heat until meat is browned and vegetables are tender. Drain excess fat.

Add tomato sauce, beef broth, chili powder, garlic powder, paprika and cumin to meat mixture; stir well. Bring to a boil over high heat. Reduce heat and let simmer, uncovered, 20 minutes; stirring occasionally.

Stir in beans, *Coca-Cola* and hot pepper sauce. Continue to simmer 10 to 15 minutes. Season to taste with salt and black pepper. Garnish as desired. Serve immediately.

TIP

Try cooking this chili one day in advance. By cooking the day before, letting it cool, then refrigerating overnight, you give all the flavors in the chili time to blend.

FRENCH LENTIL SOUP

MAKES 4 TO 6 SERVINGS

3 tablespoons olive oil

1 medium onion, chopped

1 carrot, chopped

1 stalk celery, chopped

1 clove garlic, minced

½ pound dried lentils, rinsed and sorted

1 can (about 14 ounces) stewed tomatoes mixed with ½ cup *Coca-Cola*®

3 to 4 cups chicken broth

3 tablespoons olive oil

Salt and black pepper

½ cup grated Parmesan cheese (optional)

Heat oil in large skillet over medium heat. Stir in onion, carrot, celery and garlic. Cook about 9 minutes or until vegetables are tender but not browned.

Add remaining ingredients, except cheese. Bring to a boil over high heat, reduce heat; cover and simmer 30 minutes or until tender.

Season as desired with salt and pepper. Serve in bowls or over pasta, rice or sautéed fresh spinach. Sprinkle with Parmesan cheese, if desired, just before serving.

STARTERS & SOUPS

COCA-COLA® GLAZED BACON-WRAPPED DATES

MAKES 8 SERVINGS (2 EACH)

8 slices bacon

2 tablespoons balsamic vinegar

⅓ cup *Coca-Cola®*

1 teaspoon Dijon mustard

⅛ teaspoon garlic powder

16 large dates

8 teaspoons cream cheese, divided

16 raw almonds, roasted or smoked

½ teaspoon salt

½ teaspoon black pepper

1 tablespoon unsalted butter

Preheat oven to 400°F. Cut bacon slices in half and cook in medium skillet over medium heat 1 minute on each side. Drain on paper towel and set aside. (Bacon should be soft.) Discard bacon grease.

Add vinegar, *Coca-Cola*, mustard and garlic powder to skillet. Cook on medium heat 3 to 4 minutes or until mixture becomes a thickened glaze.

While glaze is cooking, slice one side of each date lengthwise and remove pit. Fill each date with ½ teaspoon cream cheese and 1 almond, then pinch date closed.

Wrap each stuffed date with ½ slice bacon and secure with wooden toothpicks. Remove glaze from heat and stir in salt, pepper and butter. In two nonstick rimmed baking sheets, drizzle 1 tablespoon sauce and place 8 dates side by side in each.

Evenly drizzle remaining sauce over the tops and bake 10 minutes. Remove from oven and let cool slightly, 5 minutes.

STARTERS & SOUPS

MUSHROOM-BARLEY SOUP

MAKES 6 SERVINGS

6 slices bacon

1 onion, diced

3 stalks celery, sliced

2 small carrots, peeled and sliced

10 ounces sliced mushrooms

1 teaspoon minced garlic

⅛ teaspoon red pepper flakes

4 cups beef broth

1 cup uncooked medium barley

½ cup *Coca-Cola*®

1½ cups water

Salt and black pepper

Cook bacon over medium-high heat in 4-quart saucepan about 10 minutes or until crisp and browned. Remove bacon with slotted spoon, chop into bite-sized pieces and set aside. Reserve 1 tablespoon bacon grease and discard the rest. Add onion, celery, carrots and mushrooms to saucepan. Cook about 8 minutes or until vegetables are crisp-tender. Add garlic and red pepper flakes and cook an additional 1 minute, stirring constantly.

Add remaining ingredients. Bring to a boil then cover and reduce heat to medium-low. Stir in bacon and simmer 40 minutes or until barley is tender.

TIP

Before cooking the barley, rinse it thoroughly under running water, then remove any dirt or debris you may find.

CAPRESE BRUSCHETTA
MAKES 12 SERVINGS

¼ cup balsamic vinegar

2 tablespoons *Coca-Cola*®

Garlic powder, divided

6 plum tomatoes, seeded and diced

12 large fresh basil leaves, chopped

¼ cup extra virgin olive oil emulsified* with 1 tablespoon *Coca-Cola*®

1 teaspoon salt

Black pepper

¼ cup (½ stick) softened butter

1 French baguette, cut into 24 slices

12 small balls fresh mozzarella cheese, cut in half**

Fresh basil leaves

To emulsify means to blend two or more unblendable substances such as vinegar and oil. This can easily be done with a whisk, hand blender, or food processor.

**If unavailable, may use an 8-ounce fresh mozzarella ball. Cut ball in quarters and slice each quarter into 6 slices, making 24 slices total.*

Bring vinegar, *Coca-Cola* and pinch of garlic powder to a boil over medium-high heat in small saucepan. Reduce heat to medium-low and cook about 10 to 15 minutes or until mixture is reduced to a syrup. Remove mixture from heat to cool.

Meanwhile, lightly toss tomatoes with chopped basil in medium bowl. Stir in emulsified oil/*Coca-Cola* and season with salt and pepper.

Microwave butter in small microwave-safe dish 15 to 20 seconds. Spread baguette slices with butter and sprinkle lightly with garlic powder. Toast baguette slices on baking sheet under broiler about 1 minute on each side or until crisp. To serve, top bread slices with 1 heaping tablespoon of tomato/basil mixture and 2 cheese halves. Drizzle with cooled syrup and garnish with basil leaves.

STARTERS & SOUPS

BLACK BEAN DIP

MAKES 10 TO 12 SERVINGS

1½ tablespoons oil

1 shallot, minced

2 cans (15 ounces each) black beans

1 can (4½ ounces) chopped mild green chiles

1 tablespoon minced chipotle peppers

½ cup *Coca-Cola*®

⅓ cup ketchup

1 teaspoon garlic powder

1 teaspoon onion powder

¼ to ½ teaspoon ground red pepper

½ cup cream cheese

½ cup spreadable Cheddar cheese

½ cup (4 ounces) shredded sharp Cheddar cheese

Chopped green onions

Tortilla chips (optional)

Salsa (optional)

Sour cream (optional)

Preheat oven to 375°F. Heat oil in large saucepan over low heat. Add shallot; cook until softened.

Stir in black beans, chiles, chipotle peppers, *Coca-Cola* and ketchup. Add garlic powder, onion powder and ground red pepper. Bring to a boil over medium-high heat; reduce and simmer, uncovered, 25 minutes or until most liquid is evaporated, stirring frequently.

Using a fork or hand-held blender, lightly mash bean mixture. In bottom of 8-inch pan, mix together cream cheese and spreadable Cheddar cheese; spread mixture to corners.

Spoon bean mixture evenly over cheeses and sprinkle with shredded Cheddar cheese. Bake 10 to 15 minutes or until bubbly. Sprinkle with chopped green onions and serve with tortilla chips, salsa and sour cream, if desired.

GAZPACHO WITH COCA-COLA® REDUCTION

MAKES 4 TO 6 SERVINGS

⅔ cup *Coca-Cola®*, divided

½ cup balsamic vinegar, divided

¼ cup olive oil

⅔ cup tomato or vegetable juice

⅛ teaspoon ground red pepper

3 tomatoes, chopped

1 red bell pepper, chopped

1 medium sweet onion

1 large shallot, chopped

1 large cucumber, seeded and chopped

Salt and black pepper

½ cup sour cream or plain yogurt

½ cup fresh basil leaves

Bring half of *Coca-Cola* and half of vinegar to a boil over medium-high heat in medium saucepan. Cook about 3 minutes or until liquid measures about 2 tablespoons.

Meanwhile, whisk together remaining *Coca-Cola*, remaining vinegar, oil, tomato juice and ground red pepper in small bowl. Pulse tomatoes, bell pepper, onion, shallot, cucumber and tomato juice mixture together in food processor or blender until mixture becomes a rough purée. (Work in batches, if necessary.)

Season with salt and black pepper and chill several hours. Serve gazpacho in chilled bowls with dollop of sour cream. Drizzle with cooled syrup and garnish with basil.

STARTERS & SOUPS

CROSTINI WITH EGGPLANT TAPENADE

MAKES 8 SERVINGS

3 tablespoons olive oil

2 cups diced eggplant

⅓ cup diced shallots or onion

1 cup pitted kalamata olives, chopped

1 tablespoon capers with juice

½ cup red peppadew peppers, chopped with 2 tablespoons juice*

1 tablespoon balsamic vinegar

½ cup *Coca-Cola*®

½ teaspoon red pepper flakes

Salt and black pepper

Toasted baguette slices

If unavailable, may substitute with roasted red peppers.

Heat oil in large nonstick skillet over medium-high heat. Add eggplant and shallots; cook about 6 minutes or until richly golden, stirring often. Add olives, capers and peppadew peppers with their juices; continue stirring about 5 minutes or until most liquid has evaporated.

When mixture has reduced, add vinegar and *Coca-Cola*. Sprinkle with red pepper flakes, salt and black pepper.

Reduce heat to low. Cook about 15 minutes or until thickened. Stir several times during final cooking stage. Serve warm or cold on toasted baguette slices.

TIP

This versatile eggplant tapenade can also be served on top of crackers or with raw crudités.

MINI SLIDERS WITH COCA-COLA®
CARAMELIZED SHALLOTS

MAKES 12 SLIDERS

1½ pounds ground beef

1 tablespoon onion powder

1 tablespoon steak sauce

1 teaspoon salt

1 teaspoon black pepper

2 tablespoons butter

1 tablespoon olive oil

8 large shallots, thinly sliced

¼ cup *Coca-Cola*®

12 buns or mini rolls, lightly toasted

Cheddar cheese (optional)

Mix ground beef with next 4 ingredients. Form into 12 small, even patties. Set aside.

Heat butter and oil together in medium skillet over medium heat. When butter is melted, stir in shallots. Cook until just beginning to caramelize, then add *Coca-Cola*.

Increase heat to medium-high and cook liquid about 4 minutes or until liquid has almost evaporated. Return to low heat and continue cooking until fully caramelized. (Do not allow shallots to burn.)

While shallots are cooking, cook burgers in large nonstick skillet over medium-high heat 3 minutes on each side. Top each patty with slice of cheese, if desired.

Fill each bun with a burger and heaping spoonful of shallots.

HICKORY-SMOKED BARBECUE CHICKEN WINGS

MAKES 24 APPETIZERS

2 pounds chicken wings, tips removed and split in half

3 teaspoons hickory flavor liquid smoke, divided

1 cup barbecue sauce

1 cup *Coca-Cola®*

⅓ cup honey

¼ cup ketchup

2 teaspoons spicy mustard

2 teaspoons hot pepper sauce

1 teaspoon Worcestershire sauce

¼ cup sliced green onions (optional)

Place wings in large resealable food storage bag; add 2 teaspoons liquid smoke. Toss to coat. Refrigerate at least 1 hour to let flavors blend.

Preheat oven to 375°F. Spray 13×9-inch baking pan with nonstick cooking spray.

Combine barbecue sauce, *Coca-Cola*, honey, ketchup, mustard, hot pepper sauce, Worcestershire sauce and remaining 1 teaspoon liquid smoke in medium bowl; mix well. Pour sauce into prepared pan. Add wings to pan; toss to coat.

Bake 35 to 40 minutes or until wings are tender and no longer pink, basting occasionally with sauce and turning once.

Remove pan from oven and discard sauce, leaving just enough to coat wings. Set oven to broil and return wings to oven. Broil 3 to 4 minutes. Garnish with green onions, if desired, just before serving.

BEEF & PORK

LIMELIGHT STEAK BBQ

MAKES 2 SERVINGS

2 large T-bone steaks (or other select cut suitable for barbecuing)

MARINADE

2 teaspoons seasoning salt or steak seasoning

Fresh ground black pepper

3 tablespoons Worcestershire sauce

6 cloves fresh minced garlic

2 cans (12 ounces each) *Coca-Cola*®

Using a fork, pierce each steak several times on both sides and place in a shallow glass baking pan. (Do not use stainless steel.)

Sprinkle steaks with seasoning salt and fresh ground black pepper. Pour Worcestershire sauce over steaks and add garlic. Turn steaks over to ensure they are well coated with seasonings.

Pour *Coca-Cola* over steaks to completely cover. Cover pan with plastic wrap. Refrigerate for 2 hours, turning steaks after the first hour. Discard marinade and grill steaks to desired doneness.

MARINATED PORK TENDERLOIN

MAKES 4 TO 6 SERVINGS

1 cup *Coca-Cola*®

¼ cup beef broth

2 tablespoons cider vinegar

1 tablespoon honey mustard

2 small Granny Smith apples, chopped

4 to 6 green onions, finely chopped

2 cloves garlic, minced

1 teaspoon ground cinnamon

½ teaspoon ground ginger

Salt and black pepper

1 to 1½ pounds whole pork tenderloin

Combine *Coca-Cola*, beef broth, vinegar and mustard in large bowl; mix well. Add apples, onions, garlic, cinnamon, ginger, salt and black pepper to *Coca-Cola* mixture; mix well.

Place pork tenderloin in large plastic resealable food storage bag. Pour *Coca-Cola* mixture over pork, turning to coat. Seal bag and marinate in refrigerator at least 3 hours to let flavors blend, turning occasionally.

Preheat oven to 350°F. Remove pork from marinade, discard marinade. Place pork in roasting pan. Cook pork about 25 to 30 minutes or until internal temperature reaches 165°F when tested with meat thermometer inserted into thickest part of pork.

Remove pork from oven and transfer to cutting board. Let stand 10 to 15 minutes before carving. Internal temperature will continue to rise 5°F to 10°F during stand time. Serve with applesauce and your favorite side dishes.

COCA-COLA® HAM

MAKES 6 SERVINGS

½ ham (5 to 6 pounds)
1 cup packed brown sugar
1½ cups *Coca-Cola®*

1 cup crushed pineapple (optional)

Wash ham thoroughly. Rub fat side with brown sugar.

Pour *Coca-Cola* over ham. Pour crushed pineapple over ham, if desired. Bake at 450°F for 3 hours.

MATCHLESS MEATLOAF

MAKES 4 TO 6 SERVINGS

1½ pounds ground beef

1½ cups fresh bread crumbs

¼ cup minced onion

2 tablespoons finely cut parsley

1 egg

½ cup *Coca-Cola*®

2 tablespoons ketchup

1½ tablespoons prepared mustard

1 teaspoon salt

½ teaspoon basil leaves

⅛ teaspoon black pepper

In bowl, break up meat with fork; add bread crumbs, onion and parsley, mixing well. Beat egg, mix with remaining ingredients in a separate bowl. Pour over meat. With fork, toss lightly to blend thoroughly. Mixture will be soft.

Turn into a 9×5×3-inch loaf pan. Bake at 350°F for 1 hour. Let set about 10 minutes before slicing.

BEEF & PORK

ASIAN BEEF STIR FRY

MAKES 4 SERVINGS

1½ pounds beef flank steak

1 can (12 ounces) *Coca-Cola*®

1 cup beef broth

3 tablespoons soy sauce

1 teaspoon sesame oil

2 cloves garlic, minced

3 tablespoons peanut oil, divided

1 yellow bell pepper, cut into thin strips

1 red bell pepper, cut into thin strips

4 green onions, sliced diagonally

1 cup water chestnuts

1 tablespoon cornstarch

2 cups hot cooked rice

Cut steak in half lengthwise, then crosswise into ⅛-inch strips. Place strips in large resealable food storage bag. Add *Coca-Cola,* beef broth, soy sauce, sesame oil and garlic; seal bag and turn to coat. Marinate at least 3 hours or overnight in refrigerator, turning occasionally.

Remove steak from bag; reserve half of marinade in medium bowl. Heat wok or skillet over high heat or until hot. Drizzle 2 tablespoons peanut oil into work; heat 30 seconds. Add half of steak; stir-fry 2 minutes or until steak is browned and no longer pink. Repeat with remaining steak; set aside.

Reduce heat to medium-high and add remaining 1 tablespoon peanut oil; heat 30 seconds. Add bell peppers, onions and water chestnuts; cook and stir 3 minutes or until vegetables are tender; remove and set aside.

Stir cornstarch into reserved marinade until smooth. Stir marinade into wok and boil 1 minute, stirring constantly. Return steak and vegetables to wok; cook 3 minutes or until heated through. Serve over rice.

BEEF & PORK

BEEF BRISKET

MAKES 6 SERVINGS

Center-cut beef brisket (about 3 to 4 pounds)

1 packet instant onion soup mix

2 cans (4 ounces each) tomato sauce

Ground ginger

1 bottle (2 liters) *Coca-Cola*®, divided

14 to 16 new potatoes

22 to 24 small peeled carrots

In flat roasting pan, place beef brisket fat-side up.

Sprinkle onion soup mix on top of brisket; pour 2 cans of tomato sauce on top. Sprinkle with ground ginger. Pour half of 2-liter bottle of *Coca-Cola* over meat.

Place whole potatoes and carrots around sides of pan. Add enough water to cover meat.

Place in 350°F oven for 3½ to 4 hours, occasionally spooning sauce over meat. If necessary, add a little more *Coca-Cola* or water to keep meat covered.

Meat is done when fork-tender. When finished, remove meat from pan and slice fat cap off top. Using an electric knife, carefully cut meat across grain into ¼-inch slices and place in casserole dish, covering with some of the sauce. Reserve some sauce to be used as gravy.

TIP

Serve with the potatoes, carrots and fresh loaf of challah (twisted egg bread) for sopping up the gravy.

FRUITED PORK CHOPS

MAKES 4 SERVINGS

4 rib, loin or shoulder pork chops or smoked pork chops, ½- to ¾-inch thick

1 teaspoon salt

⅛ teaspoon black pepper

⅛ teaspoon ground ginger

1 medium apple

1 medium lemon or orange

2 tablespoons packed brown sugar

½ cup *Coca-Cola*®

1 tablespoon cornstarch

Trim fat from chops, then brown them on each side in ungreased skillet. Lay chops in shallow baking pan. Do not overlap. Sprinkle with salt, pepper and ginger.

Core unpeeled apple, cut crosswise into 4 thick slices. Cut lemon into 4 slices; remove seeds. Lay lemon slices atop apple slices and place on each chop.

Sprinkle with brown sugar. Pour *Coca-Cola* around chops. Cover tightly. Bake in 350°F oven for 45 minutes.

Blend cornstarch with 2 tablespoons water until smooth. Stir into meat juices. Bake, uncovered, 15 minutes longer or until meat is fork-tender. Spoon sauce over fruit chops to glaze.

BEEF & PORK

SPICY PORK PO' BOYS

MAKES 4 SERVINGS

1 tablespoon paprika

1 tablespoon garlic powder

1 tablespoon onion powder

2 tablespoons chili powder

1 teaspoon ground red pepper

½ to 1 tablespoon salt

1 tablespoon black pepper

1 pound boneless pork ribs

½ cup *Coca-Cola®*

1 tablespoon hot pepper sauce

Dash Worcestershire sauce

½ cup ketchup

4 French rolls, toasted

½ cup prepared coleslaw

Mix dry ingredients together to create a rub and coat ribs well on all sides. Let ribs sit at least 3 hours or overnight.

Place ribs in covered ceramic dish or Dutch oven. Combine *Coca-Cola*, hot pepper sauce and Worcestershire sauce in small bowl; drizzle evenly over pork.

Bake, covered, at 250°F at least 4 hours. (Pork should easily fall apart.)

Remove pork from dish or Dutch oven. Add ketchup to sauce in dish and cook 4 to 6 minutes or until sauce has thickened and combined. Pour sauce over pork and break apart with two forks while mixing in sauce.

Serve pork on toasted French rolls topped with coleslaw.

TIP

Instead of topping with coleslaw, you can also top with shredded lettuce, tomatoes or pickles.

BEEF & PORK

CHERRY PORK MEDALLIONS WITH COCA-COLA®

MAKES 4 SERVINGS

1 pound pork tenderloin

1 tablespoon olive oil

1 jar (10 ounces) cherry preserves

¼ cup *Coca-Cola*®

2 tablespoons light corn syrup

¼ teaspoon ground cinnamon

¼ teaspoon ground nutmeg

¼ teaspoon ground cloves

¼ teaspoon salt

Slice tenderloin into ½-inch-thick medallions. Heat oil in large nonstick skillet over medium heat, add pork and cook about 2 minutes each side. Remove pork from skillet; set aside.

Combine cherry preserves, *Coca-Cola*, corn syrup, cinnamon, nutmeg, cloves and salt in same skillet. Bring to a boil over medium-high heat, stirring constantly, about 3 minutes.

Return pork to skillet; cover and simmer 8 to 10 minutes or until pork is cooked through.

NOTE

This recipe uses pork tenderloin with a sweet, savory sauce—perfect for a quick weeknight dish or as an easy weekend meal.

SMOKEHOUSE BARBECUED BRISKET

MAKES 6 SERVINGS

3 tablespoons olive oil

1 beef brisket, trimmed (about 3 to 4 pounds)

Salt and black pepper

1 tablespoon garlic powder

1 cup beef broth

1 onion, minced

1 teaspoon red pepper flakes

1 tablespoon liquid smoke

½ cup *Coca-Cola*®

4 tablespoons packed dark brown sugar, divided

2 cups tomato purée

1 can (12 ounces) *Coca-Cola*®

2 tablespoons onion powder

2 tablespoons hot pepper sauce

1 tablespoon Worcestershire sauce

Kaiser rolls or hamburger buns

Preheat oven to 250°F. Heat oil in large skillet over medium-high heat. While heating, season brisket liberally with salt, black pepper and garlic powder.

Brown brisket in skillet about 4 to 5 minutes on each side; remove to large covered casserole or Dutch oven.

Deglaze skillet with broth, scraping bottom of pan. Add onion, red pepper flakes and liquid smoke. When onion is translucent, add ½ cup *Coca-Cola.* Pour mixture over meat; sprinkle with 2 tablespoons brown sugar.

Braise brisket 5 to 6 hours, basting every ½ hour. When falling apart, remove meat; set aside to cool slightly and add remaining 2 tablespoons brown sugar, tomato purée, 1 can *Coca-Cola,* onion powder, hot pepper sauce and Worcestershire sauce to casserole. *Increase heat to 400°F.* Cook, uncovered, 30 minutes. When cool enough, slice meat into ½-inch slices. Return brisket to casserole and baste with sauce. *Reduce heat to 250°F.* Cook 30 minutes more. Serve as is or on rolls.

BEEF & PORK

COCA-COLA® SLOPPY JOES

MAKES 4 TO 6 SERVINGS

1 pound ground beef

1 onion, finely chopped

¾ cup finely chopped green bell pepper

1½ tablespoons all-purpose flour

1 cup *Coca-Cola®*

½ cup ketchup

2 tablespoons vinegar

1 tablespoon Worcestershire sauce

2 teaspoons dry mustard

½ teaspoon black pepper

½ teaspoon salt

Hamburger buns

Brown ground beef, onion and bell pepper in heavy-bottomed saucepan over medium heat. When meat is cooked through, drain excess fat.

Add remaining ingredients, except buns, and stir to combine. Cover and simmer 30 minutes, stirring occasionally.

Serve meat mixture on hamburger buns.

NOTE

This family-favorite recipe usually includes ground beef, ketchup or tomato sauce and a variety of spices served between two slices of bread or on a bun. Sloppy Joes are easy to prepare and budget-friendly.

BEEF & PORK

SWEET AND SOUR GLAZED BEEF KEBOBS

MAKES 6 SERVINGS

- ¾ cup *Coca-Cola*®, divided
- ½ cup pineapple juice
- ¼ cup soy sauce
- ⅓ cup cider vinegar
- 1 tablespoon Worcestershire sauce
- 1 tablespoon tomato paste
- 4 tablespoons packed dark brown sugar, divided
- 1 tablespoon garlic powder
- ½ teaspoon red pepper flakes
- 1 large onion, cut into 1-inch pieces
- 2 pounds boneless sirloin steak, cut into 1½-inch cubes
- 2½ teaspoons cornstarch
- 2 to 3 teaspoons chili-garlic sauce*
- Salt and black pepper
- Hot cooked white rice (optional)

Chili-garlic sauce can be found in the Asian foods section of the grocery store.

Mix ½ cup *Coca-Cola*, pineapple juice, soy sauce, vinegar, Worcestershire sauce, tomato paste, 2 tablespoons brown sugar, garlic powder, red pepper flakes and onion in covered container; marinate steak overnight in refrigerator.

Remove steak cubes and onion pieces. Reserve marinade.

Add marinade to small saucepan. Bring to a boil over high heat. Spoon 2 tablespoons marinade into small bowl and stir cornstarch into hot liquid until mixture is smooth. Return liquid to pan. Stir in remaining 2 tablespoons brown sugar and chili-garlic sauce. Reduce heat to medium and simmer 15 to 18 minutes until thickened and reduced to 1 cup. Season with salt and black pepper.

Meanwhile, place steak cubes on 6 skewers, alternating evenly with onion pieces. Broil 3 minutes, turn and broil 2 minutes.

Glaze kabobs with sauce using a clean pastry brush. Serve over rice, if desired.

BEEF & PORK

NOTE

If using wooden skewers, soak them in water for 20 minutes to prevent them from burning during the cooking process.

BEEF & PORK

SPAGHETTI AND MEATBALLS

MAKES 4 TO 6 SERVINGS

3 slices day-old Italian bread, torn into small pieces

⅓ cup *Coca-Cola®* mixed with 1 tablespoon balsamic vinegar

1½ pounds ground beef or a combination of ground beef, veal and pork

1 medium yellow onion, finely diced

¼ cup chopped fresh parsley mixed with ¼ cup minced fresh basil

1 egg

1½ cups grated Parmesan cheese, divided, plus additional if desired

2 cans (about 14 ounces each) diced tomatoes, undrained and divided

1½ teaspoons dried oregano, divided

3 to 4 cups cooked spaghetti

Preheat oven to 350°F. Soak bread in *Coca-Cola* mixture and heat in microwave on HIGH 30 seconds. Mash with a fork.

Mix beef, onion, herb mixture, egg and 1 cup Parmesan cheese together in large mixing bowl; add mashed bread. Mix until incorporated. Form meat mixture into 12 large or 18 smaller meatballs; refrigerate 15 to 30 minutes to firm.

Coat large skillet with nonstick cooking spray; heat over medium heat. Add meatballs; cook 8 to 10 minutes or until browned on all sides. Remove from heat.

Pour two thirds of tomatoes over the bottom of large rectangular baking dish. Season with half of oregano. Sprinkle with ¼ cup Parmesan cheese.

Gently set meatballs in rows ½ inch apart in prepared dish. Drizzle with remaining tomatoes; sprinkle with remaining oregano and Parmesan cheese. Bake 40 to 45 minutes. Serve over cooked spaghetti. Garnish with additional cheese, if desired.

BEEF & PORK

CHICKEN & SEAFOOD

APRICOT COCA-COLA® AND ROSEMARY CHICKEN

MAKES 4 SERVINGS

4 boneless skinless chicken breasts

2 cloves garlic, minced

¼ teaspoon kosher salt

¼ teaspoon red pepper flakes

4 tablespoons apricot preserves

½ cup *Coca-Cola®*

¼ cup low-sodium soy sauce

2 tablespoons chopped fresh rosemary, plus additional for garnish

Place chicken in large baking dish. Rub garlic, salt and red pepper flakes over chicken. Spread 1 tablespoon apricot preserves over each chicken breast. Drizzle with *Coca-Cola* and soy sauce; sprinkle with 2 tablespoons rosemary. Cover and marinate at room temperature at least 30 minutes.

Preheat grill to medium-high heat. Remove chicken from marinade; discard marinade. Grill chicken on lightly greased grill grid coated with nonstick cooking spray 5 minutes on each side or until chicken is cooked through. Serve immediately and garnish with fresh rosemary.

COUNTRY CAPTAIN CHICKEN

MAKES 4 TO 6 SERVINGS

¼ cup olive oil

4 boneless skinless chicken breast halves

1 medium onion, sliced

1 medium green bell pepper, sliced

1 can (14½ ounces) chicken broth

1 cup *Coca-Cola*®

1 can (14½ ounces) whole tomatoes, undrained and coarsely chopped

1 can (6 ounces) tomato paste

1 teaspoon hot pepper sauce

½ teaspoon ground white pepper

1 bay leaf

2 tablespoons fresh parsley leaves, chopped

2 cups hot cooked rice

Heat oil in large skillet over medium-high heat. Add chicken breasts; cook 3 to 4 minutes on each side or until lightly browned. Remove from skillet; set aside.

Add onion and bell pepper to skillet. Cook and stir 5 minutes or until vegetables are tender. Add chicken broth and *Coca-Cola* to skillet, scraping up any browned bits from bottom of pan. Add tomatoes, tomato paste, hot pepper sauce, white pepper and bay leaf. Cook and stir 5 minutes or until sauce thickens slightly.

Return chicken to pan and simmer, uncovered, about 15 minutes or until chicken is no longer pink in center.

Remove chicken breasts to serving platter. Remove bay leaf from sauce. Pour sauce over chicken and garnish with parsley. Serve over rice.

CHICKEN & SEAFOOD

CASSEROLE BBQ CHICKEN

MAKES 4 TO 6 SERVINGS

3 pounds cut-up whole chicken or chicken breasts, thighs and legs

⅓ cup all-purpose flour

2 teaspoons salt

⅓ cup oil

½ cup onion, finely diced

½ cup celery, finely diced

½ cup green bell pepper, finely diced

1 cup ketchup

1 cup *Coca-Cola*®*

2 tablespoons Worcestershire sauce

1 tablespoon salt

½ teaspoon hickory smoked salt

½ teaspoon dried basil leaves

½ teaspoon chili powder

⅛ teaspoon black pepper

*To reduce foam for accurate measurement, use Coca-Cola at room temperature and stir rapidly.

Rinse chicken pieces; pat dry. Coat chicken with flour and salt. Brown pieces on all sides in hot oil, then place pieces in a 3-quart casserole. (Discard drippings.)

Combine remaining ingredients, mixing well. Spoon sauce over chicken, covering all pieces. Cover casserole; bake at 350°F about 1¼ hours or until chicken is fork-tender.

CHICKEN & SEAFOOD

TERIYAKI CHICKEN

MAKES 4 TO 6 SERVINGS

1 pound skinless boneless chicken breasts, cut into strips

MARINADE

1 cup soy sauce

½ cup *Coca-Cola*®

2 tablespoons orange juice

1 tablespoon fresh ginger, minced

1 clove garlic, minced

Salt, black pepper and chili powder to taste

¼ cup vegetable oil

Combine all marinade ingredients and marinate chicken overnight.

Place chicken on well-oiled pan and bake at 350°F for about 30 minutes. Remove from oven, slide chicken around in pan to sop up caramelized sauce, baste with additional marinade and return to oven for another 15 minutes.

TIP

If you have any chicken left over, simply combine it with mixed greens, sliced bell peppers, green onion and cucumber for a delicious and healthful teriyaki chicken salad.

CHICKEN & SEAFOOD

BALSAMIC COCA-COLA® CHICKEN

MAKES 4 SERVINGS

½ cup chopped shallots

2 tablespoons olive oil, divided

1 cup *Coca-Cola*®

⅓ cup balsamic vinegar

1½ pounds boneless skinless chicken cutlets

2 cloves garlic, minced

2 tablespoons chopped fresh basil leaves

½ teaspoon salt

½ teaspoon black pepper

Fresh basil leaves (optional)

Preheat grill to medium-high heat.

Cook shallots in 1 tablespoon oil in large nonstick skillet over medium heat 3 minutes or until tender. Add *Coca-Cola* and vinegar; simmer over low heat 10 minutes or until reduced to ⅔ cup. Reserve ¼ cup in separate bowl and set aside.

Place chicken on nonstick baking sheet. Rub with garlic, chopped basil, salt and pepper; drizzle with remaining oil.

Grill chicken on a lightly greased grill grid coated with nonstick cooking spray 2 to 3 minutes on each side or until chicken is done, basting with reserved ¼ cup *Coca-Cola*/balsamic mixture. Serve immediately with remaining balsamic mixture. Garnish with fresh basil, if desired.

TIP

Be sure to use chicken cutlets in this recipe. Chicken cutlets are boneless, skinless sections of the chicken breast which have been tenderized. Cutlets cook quicker than chicken breasts.

CHICKEN & SEAFOOD

SEARED SCALLOPS WITH COCA-COLA® GLAZE

MAKES 4 SERVINGS

1 tablespoon butter

1¼ pounds sea scallops, rinsed and dried well

2 tablespoons *Coca-Cola®*

1 tablespoon dry white wine

1 teaspoon soy sauce

1 teaspoon packed brown sugar

Heat butter in large skillet over medium-high heat. Add scallops; cook 2 to 3 minutes on each side or until scallops are opaque. Remove scallops to plate.

Add *Coca-Cola*, wine, soy sauce and brown sugar to skillet; cook 20 to 30 seconds or until liquid thickens. Add scallops; heat through and glaze. Serve immediately.

CHICKEN & SEAFOOD

SWEET SOUTHERN BARBECUE CHICKEN

MAKES 4 SERVINGS

2 to 3 tablespoons oil, divided

½ cup chopped onion

1 clove garlic, minced

½ cup packed brown sugar

1 teaspoon dry mustard

1 tablespoon honey mustard

1 tablespoon Dijon mustard

1 cup *Coca-Cola*®

2 tablespoons balsamic vinegar

2 tablespoons cider vinegar

2 tablespoons Worcestershire sauce

½ cup ketchup

2 to 3 pounds boneless skinless chicken thighs

SAUCE

Heat 1 tablespoon oil in medium skillet over medium heat. Add onion and garlic and cook 2 minutes.

Add next 4 ingredients; bring to a boil over medium-high heat, reduce heat and simmer, uncovered, 20 minutes or until sauce thickens.

Add *Coca-Cola*, balsamic vinegar, cider vinegar, Worcestershire sauce and ketchup; stir.

Simmer 15 to 20 minutes until sauce thickens. Remove from heat.

CHICKEN

Heat remaining oil in large skillet over medium-high heat. Add half of chicken and cook about 5 to 7 minutes per side or until cooked through. After turning, brush chicken with barbecue sauce. Brush both sides again with sauce in the last 1 to 2 minutes of cooking. Serve chicken with additional sauce. Repeat with remaining chicken.

SEAFOOD GRATIN

MAKES 6 SERVINGS

½ pound cooked shrimp

½ pound cooked crabmeat

½ pound cooked sole

½ pound cooked lobster

2 tablespoons butter

2 tablespoons all-purpose flour

½ cup milk

¾ cup grated Parmesan cheese

½ cup *Coca-Cola*®

Bread crumbs or panko bread crumbs

Preheat oven to 325°F. Cut seafood into bite-sized pieces; place in greased baking dish.

Melt butter in small saucepan. Add flour, whisking constantly to form a roux. When roux is lightly browned, stir in milk and Parmesan cheese. When mixture is slightly thickened, add *Coca-Cola*.

Pour sauce over seafood and top with bread crumbs. Bake gratin 20 to 25 minutes. Remove from oven to cool slightly before serving.

CREOLE SHRIMP

MAKES 4 SERVINGS

2 tablespoons olive oil

½ cup diced green bell pepper

½ cup diced onion

½ cup diced celery

1 teaspoon chili powder

1 can (about 14 ounces) diced tomatoes, undrained

1 can (8 ounces) tomato sauce

½ cup *Coca-Cola®*

1 tablespoon hot pepper sauce

1 tablespoon Worcestershire sauce

Salt and black pepper

1½ pounds raw medium shrimp, peeled and deveined

Hot cooked rice

2 green onions, sliced

Heat oil in stockpot or Dutch oven. Add bell pepper, onion and celery; cook and stir until onion is soft and translucent. Add chili powder; stir to coat vegetables.

Add tomatoes, tomato sauce, *Coca-Cola*, hot pepper sauce and Worcestershire sauce. Season with salt and black pepper. Simmer on low heat about 45 minutes, stirring occasionally, or until thickened.

Add shrimp to mixture; stir well. Continue simmering 15 minutes. Serve over hot cooked rice and garnish with green onions.

TIP

For a healthier variation, add additional vegetables like zucchini and red bell pepper and serve over brown rice.

CHICKEN & SEAFOOD

HOISIN CHICKEN

MAKES 4 SERVINGS

½ cup *Coca-Cola*®

¼ cup soy sauce

2 tablespoons hoisin sauce

2 cloves garlic, minced

1 teaspoon freshly grated ginger

¼ teaspoon red pepper flakes

1½ pounds boneless skinless chicken cutlets

Whisk together *Coca-Cola*, soy sauce, hoisin sauce, garlic, ginger and red pepper flakes in medium bowl; set aside.

Place chicken in large resealable food storage bag. Pour *Coca-Cola* mixture over chicken; cover and refrigerate at least 30 minutes or overnight.

Preheat grill to medium-high heat.

Remove chicken from marinade; discard marinade. Grill half of chicken on lightly greased grill grid coated with nonstick cooking spray 2 to 3 minutes on each side or until chicken is done. Repeat with remaining chicken.

SHRIMP AND SCALLOP FETTUCCINE

MAKES 4 TO 6 SERVINGS

1 tablespoon butter

1 small onion, chopped

½ pound sea scallops

½ pound raw medium shrimp, peeled and deveined

½ pound mushrooms, sliced

½ cup *Coca-Cola*®

½ cup water

1 tablespoon freshly squeezed lemon juice

3 tablespoons all-purpose flour

1 teaspoon salt

1 cup half-and-half

1 pound spinach fettuccine, cooked

3 tablespoons shredded Parmesan cheese (optional)

2 tablespoons chopped fresh parsley (optional)

Melt butter in large skillet over medium heat. Add onion; cook until softened and translucent.

Add scallops, shrimp, mushrooms, *Coca-Cola,* water and lemon juice to skillet. Reduce heat to medium-low. Cover and cook until scallops are opaque and shrimp are tender, stirring frequently.

Meanwhile, blend flour, salt and half-and-half in small bowl. Gradually add flour mixture to seafood mixture, stirring constantly, until thickened and combined.

Divide fettuccine among serving bowls. Spoon seafood mixture over pasta; garnish with Parmesan cheese and parsley.

NOTE

There are two types of scallops available: sea scallops and bay scallops. Sea scallops are more widely available although they're less tender. Bay scallops are smaller, slightly sweeter and more expensive.

CHICKEN & SEAFOOD

COCA-COLA®-MARINATED SPANISH CHICKEN

MAKES 4 SERVINGS

1½ pounds bone-in chicken breasts

2 tablespoons dried oregano

2 cloves garlic, minced

½ teaspoon salt

½ teaspoon black pepper

½ cup pimiento-stuffed green olives

⅓ cup capers

1¼ cups *Coca-Cola*®

⅓ cup red wine vinegar

2 tablespoons olive oil

1½ teaspoons paprika

2 tablespoons chopped fresh parsley

Preheat oven to 350°F. Season chicken with oregano, garlic, salt and pepper. Place chicken in shallow dish or resealable plastic bag. Add olives and capers.

Combine *Coca-Cola*, vinegar and oil in small bowl; pour over chicken. Cover and marinate at least 1 hour or up to 8 hours.

Arrange chicken mixture in 13×9-inch baking dish and spoon marinade over chicken. Sprinkle both sides of chicken with paprika.

Cover and bake chicken 50 minutes to 1 hour until chicken is cooked through. Serve with additional olives, capers and chopped fresh parsley.

TIP

Capers are deep green flower buds of a Mediterranean bush that have been preserved in a vinegary brine. Rinse them in cold water to remove excess salt before using.

SWEET AND SPICY SHRIMP TACOS WITH MANGO SALSA

MAKES 6 SERVINGS

1½ pounds raw shrimp, peeled and deveined

1 teaspoon salt

1 teaspoon granulated sugar

½ cup *Coca-Cola*®

⅓ cup chili sauce

2 tablespoons packed brown sugar

1 tablespoon lime juice

1 teaspoon hot pepper sauce

1 tablespoon chopped fresh cilantro

6 lightly grilled flour tortillas

Mango Salsa (recipe follows)

Place shrimp in medium bowl; sprinkle with salt and granulated sugar. Stir to coat and refrigerate 30 minutes.

Meanwhile, heat *Coca-Cola*, chili sauce, brown sugar, lime juice and hot pepper sauce in small skillet over medium heat until sauce begins to simmer and thicken. Remove from heat; stir in cilantro and set aside. Prepare Mango Salsa.

Cook shrimp in large skillet over medium-high heat 3 minutes or until shrimp are pink and opaque.

Drizzle sauce over cooked shrimp and serve in flour tortillas topped with Mango Salsa.

CHICKEN & SEAFOOD

MANGO SALSA

2 mangoes, pitted and chopped

1 cucumber, peeled, seeded and chopped

1 red or yellow bell pepper, seeded and chopped

1 jalapeño pepper*, seeded and finely chopped

¼ cup diced red onion

1 clove garlic, minced

2 tablespoons chopped fresh cilantro

1 tablespoon lime juice

1 tablespoon *Coca-Cola®*

Salt and black pepper

Jalapeño peppers can sting and irritate the skin, so wear rubber gloves when handling peppers and do not touch your eyes.

Combine all ingredients in medium bowl; stir until well combined. Cover and refrigerate 1 to 4 hours before serving.

CHICKEN & SEAFOOD

SIDES, SAUCES & SALADS

UNCLE JOE'S BAKED BEANS
MAKES 4 SERVINGS

8 slices bacon, cut into
½-inch pieces

1 medium onion, chopped

1 can (12 ounces) *Coca-Cola*®

1 can (6 ounces) tomato
paste

1 tablespoon Dijon mustard

1 teaspoon hot pepper sauce

1 can (15¼ ounces) kidney
beans, drained

1 can (15 ounces) pinto
beans, drained

2 cans (8 ounces each)
crushed pineapple,
drained

Cook bacon and onion in large skillet over medium-high heat until bacon is browned and crispy. Drain fat; set aside.

Preheat oven to 375°F. Spray 11×7-inch baking dish with nonstick cooking spray.

Combine *Coca-Cola*, tomato paste, mustard and hot pepper sauce in large bowl; mix well. Add beans, pineapple and bacon mixture to *Coca-Cola* mixture; mix well. Transfer to prepared dish. Bake, uncovered, 20 to 25 minutes or until beans are hot and bubbly.

TIP
Baked beans are a real crowd-pleaser!
Serve this summer favorite alongside burgers at your
next picnic, barbecue or family gathering!

THICK BARBECUE SAUCE
MAKES 2 CUPS

2 medium onions
¾ cup *Coca-Cola*®
¾ cup ketchup
2 tablespoons vinegar

2 tablespoons
    Worcestershire sauce
½ teaspoon chili powder
½ teaspoon salt

Shred or blender-chop onions. Combine all ingredients in medium saucepan over high heat. Bring to a boil. Cover pan; reduce heat and simmer about 45 minutes or until sauce is very thick. Stir occasionally.

To serve, heat frankfurters in sauce or spoon sauce over cooked burgers.

SIDES, SAUCES & SALADS

SWEET-SOUR CABBAGE

MAKES 4 SERVINGS

1½ pounds red or green cabbage

2 medium apples

½ cup *Coca-Cola*®*

2 tablespoons vinegar

2 tablespoons packed brown sugar

2 tablespoons bacon drippings

1 teaspoon salt

½ to 1 teaspoon caraway seeds

*To reduce foam for accurate measurement, use Coca-Cola at room temperature and stir rapidly.

Coarsely shred or cut cabbage (should measure 3 cups).

Core and dice unpeeled apples. In pan, toss together cabbage, apples and all remaining ingredients.

Cover; simmer about 25 minutes or until cabbage is tender. Stir occasionally. Serve.

MUSTARD HERB DRESSING
MAKES 1¾ CUPS

1 cup oil

½ cup *Coca-Cola*®

¼ cup wine, cider vinegar or lemon juice

1 tablespoon Dijon French mustard

1½ teaspoons Italian seasoning herbs

1 teaspoon salt

½ small clove garlic, minced

Combine all ingredients in small mixing bowl. Beat until well blended.

Pour into covered glass jar. Chill several hours to blend flavors. Shake before using.

TIP

This sweet-sour Italian-style dressing keeps very well and can be used on vegetable or fruit salads.

CREAMY CARIBBEAN SHRIMP SALAD

MAKES 4 SERVINGS

1 cup mayonnaise

¼ cup cocktail sauce

¼ cup *Coca-Cola*®

1 teaspoon lime juice

½ teaspoon salt

¼ teaspoon black pepper

1 pound shrimp, cooked and cleaned

1 package (10 ounces) prepared mixed salad greens

2 ripe mangoes, peeled, pitted and sliced

½ cup chopped walnuts

Combine mayonnaise, cocktail sauce, *Coca-Cola,* lime juice, salt and pepper in small jar with tight-fitting lid. Shake well. Refrigerate until ready to use.

Combine shrimp, salad greens, mangoes and walnuts in large bowl. Divide mixture onto plates. Drizzle dressing over salads.

TIP

The unique flavors of this salad make it an out-of-the-ordinary treat for your next gathering. For an extra special summer flavor, try grilling the shrimp before adding it to the salad.

SIDES, SAUCES & SALADS

ROASTED POTATO SALAD WITH VEGETABLES

MAKES 4 TO 6 SERVINGS

4 to 5 small red potatoes, cut into 1-inch cubes (about 5 cups)

2 sweet potatoes, cut into 1-inch cubes (about 3 cups)

⅓ cup diced red onion

1 tablespoon plus 1 teaspoon olive oil

2 tablespoons *Coca-Cola*®

2 teaspoons balsamic vinegar

1 tablespoon packed brown sugar

Salt and black pepper

2 cups green beans, cut into 1-inch pieces

2 large tomatoes, seeded and chopped

1 yellow, red or orange bell pepper, chopped

DRESSING

1 tablespoon mayonnaise

3 tablespoons honey mustard

3 tablespoons *Coca-Cola*®

1 teaspoon balsamic vinegar

Preheat oven to 400°F. Mix red potatoes, sweet potatoes, onion, oil, 2 tablespoons *Coca-Cola* and vinegar on rimmed baking sheet.

Sprinkle with brown sugar, salt and black pepper and mix to coat. Roast 17 to 20 minutes until potatoes are browned and tender.

Meanwhile, steam green beans over boiling water about 3 to 4 minutes or until crisp-tender.

When potatoes and green beans are done, combine with tomatoes and bell peppers. Combine dressing ingredients and stir until all ingredients are coated. Serve hot or warm.

SIDES, SAUCES & SALADS

SICHUAN GREEN BEANS WITH MUSHROOMS

MAKES 4 SERVINGS

2 tablespoons soy sauce

2 tablespoons *Coca-Cola*®

1 teaspoon sugar

1 tablespoon honey mustard

1 teaspoon cornstarch

3 tablespoons oil, divided

1 pound green beans

8 ounces white button or shiitake mushrooms

3 cloves garlic

1 teaspoon chopped fresh ginger

1 teaspoon toasted sesame seeds (optional)

Mix soy sauce, *Coca-Cola*, sugar, mustard and cornstarch in small bowl; set aside.

Heat 2 tablespoons oil in 12-inch skillet over medium-high heat. Add green beans; stir-fry 8 to 10 minutes or until beans are crisp-tender and their skins are browned and shriveled. Transfer beans to bowl or plate.

Heat remaining 1 tablespoon oil in skillet. Add mushrooms and cook until tender, 2 to 3 minutes for button mushrooms or 4 to 5 for shiitakes. Add garlic and ginger and cook 30 seconds.

Return beans to skillet with mushrooms and add sauce. Sauce will thicken immediately; stir until beans are heated through. Sprinkle with sesame seeds, if desired.

GRILLED ROMAINE HEARTS WITH TANGY VINAIGRETTE

MAKES 6 SERVINGS, PLUS 1 QUART VINAIGRETTE

TANGY VINAIGRETTE

3 cups *Coca-Cola®*

⅓ cup white vinegar

⅓ cup canola oil

¼ cup sugar

1 teaspoon salt

½ teaspoon onion powder

½ teaspoon garlic powder

3 tablespoons ketchup

1 tablespoon balsamic vinegar

⅛ teaspoon black pepper

2 tablespoons honey mustard

ROMAINE HEARTS

6 romaine hearts

¼ to ½ cup olive oil

Salt and black pepper

Combine *Coca-Cola*, white vinegar, canola oil, sugar, 1 teaspoon salt, onion powder, garlic powder, ketchup, balsamic vinegar, ⅛ teaspoon pepper and mustard in medium bowl; set aside.

Prepare grill for direct cooking (medium-high heat). Cut romaine hearts in half lengthwise, drizzle with olive oil and sprinkle generously with salt and pepper.

Grill about 2 minutes on each side, until lightly charred and wilted.

Drizzle with Tangy Vinaigrette and serve. Refrigerate remaining vinaigrette for future use.

SIDES, SAUCES & SALADS

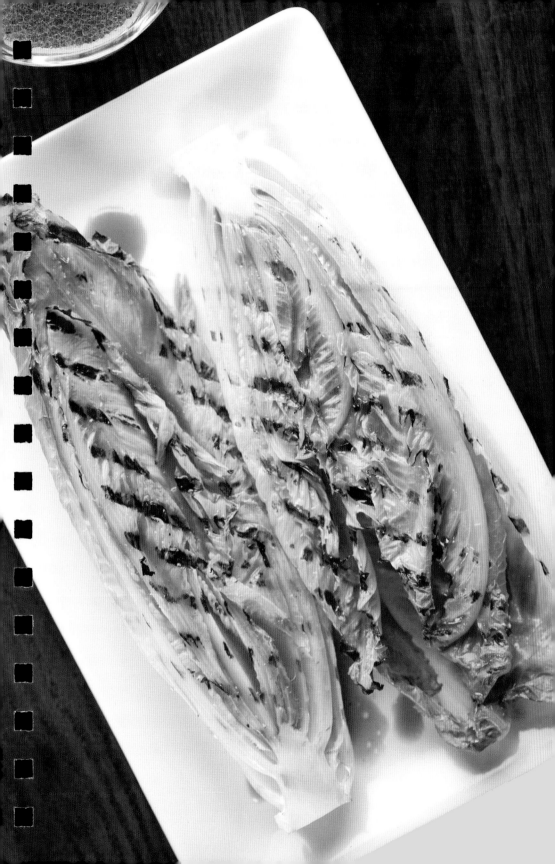

BRAISED BRUSSELS SPROUTS WITH CARAMELIZED ONIONS

MAKES 4 SERVINGS

½ tablespoon butter

1 cup diced onion

5 tablespoons *Coca-Cola*®, divided

1 teaspoon balsamic vinegar

1 pound Brussels sprouts, trimmed and halved lengthwise

3 tablespoons dry white wine, divided

Salt and black pepper

Heat butter in large skillet over medium heat. Reduce heat to medium-low and add onion; cook 10 minutes. Add 1 tablespoon *Coca-Cola* and vinegar; cook 5 minutes.

Cook Brussels sprouts in boiling water in medium saucepan, about 5 minutes; drain. Add Brussels sprouts to skillet with onions and increase heat to medium. Add 2 tablespoons wine and 2 tablespoons *Coca-Cola*; cook about 3 minutes or until most liquid has evaporated from skillet.

Add remaining 1 tablespoon wine and 2 tablespoons *Coca-Cola* to skillet; stir and cook 2 minutes or until most liquid has evaporated from pan and Brussels sprouts are tender. Season with salt and pepper.

NOTE

The caramelized onions add a tasty touch to these bright green vegetables.

MUSHROOM COCA-COLA® GRAVY
MAKES ABOUT 2 CUPS GRAVY

4 tablespoons vegetable oil

⅓ cup all-purpose flour

Salt and black pepper

1 cup beef broth

1 cup *Coca-Cola®*

1 tablespoon butter

⅓ cup onion, finely chopped

1 cup mushrooms, sliced

1½ teaspoons fresh garlic, minced

1½ teaspoons chopped fresh parsley

Heat oil in skillet over medium-high heat; add flour to create a thin roux. Sprinkle mixture with salt and pepper. Stir mixture constantly.

When roux becomes opaque, pour in broth and *Coca-Cola*, whisking constantly to avoid lumps.

Continuing to stir, reduce heat to medium-low, and let mixture bubble (do not boil) about 5 minutes or until thickened. Reduce heat further to low, cover pan and simmer 10 minutes. Continue checking on mixture and stirring as needed.

Meanwhile, melt butter in separate skillet. Add onion, mushrooms, garlic and parsley. Cook and stir until onion is translucent. Add onion mixture to *Coca-Cola* mixture. Increase heat to medium and simmer about 5 minutes or until thickened and combined.

TIP
Serve with chicken, beef, turkey or even with pasta.

SIDES, SAUCES & SALADS

COCA-COLA® CHUTNEY CARROTS

MAKES 4 SERVINGS

2 cups baby carrots

1 can (12 ounces) *Coca-Cola*®

1 cup water plus additional, as needed

3 tablespoons cranberry chutney

1 tablespoon Dijon mustard

2 teaspoons butter

2 tablespoons chopped pecans, toasted

Place carrots in medium saucepan over medium-high heat; cover with *Coca-Cola* and 1 cup water. Bring to a boil, reduce heat and simmer about 8 minutes or until carrots are tender.

Drain carrots and return to saucepan. Add chutney, mustard and butter. Cook and stir over medium-low heat until carrots are glazed.

Place carrots in serving bowl. Top with pecans.

NOTE

Mango chutney can be used in place of cranberry chutney.

DESSERTS & BEVERAGES

CHERRY AND COKE® APPLE RINGS
MAKES 4 SERVINGS

3 Granny Smith or other tart apples, peeled and cored

½ teaspoon plus ¼ teaspoon sugar-free, cherry-flavored gelatin powder

⅓ cup *Coca-Cola®*

⅓ cup nondairy whipped topping

Slice apples crosswise into ¼-inch-thick rings; remove seeds. Place stacks of apple rings in large microwavable bowl; sprinkle with gelatin. Pour *Coca-Cola* over rings.

Cover loosely with waxed paper. Microwave on HIGH 5 minutes or until liquid is boiling. Allow to stand, covered, 5 minutes. Arrange on dessert plates. Serve warm with whipped topping.

BRAZILIAN ICED CHOCOLATE

MAKES 4 TO 6 SERVINGS

2 squares (1 ounce each)
    unsweetened chocolate

¼ cup sugar

1 cup double strength hot
    coffee

2½ cups milk

1½ cups *Coca-Cola*®, chilled

Ice cream or whipped
    cream

Melt chocolate in top of double boiler over hot water. Stir in sugar. Gradually stir in hot coffee, mixing thoroughly.

Add milk and continue cooking about 10 minutes or until all particles of chocolate are dissolved and mixture is smooth. Pour into jar, cover and chill. When ready to serve, stir in chilled *Coca-Cola*. Serve over ice cubes in tall glasses. Top with ice cream or whipped cream.

TIP

To put a twist on this tasty dessert, try it with different flavors of ice cream, chopped nuts or caramel sauce.

DATE-NUT BREAD
MAKES 1 LOAF

1 package (8 ounces) pitted dates

1¼ cups *Coca-Cola*®

1 cup firmly packed light brown sugar

2 tablespoons oil

2 cups all-purpose flour

1 teaspoon baking powder

1 teaspoon baking soda

1 egg

1 teaspoon vanilla

½ cup chopped pecans or walnuts

Chop dates. Heat *Coca-Cola* to boiling. Remove from heat and stir in dates, mixing very well.

Stir in brown sugar and oil. Let cool while preparing other ingredients. Lightly spoon flour into cup to measure. Stir together flour, baking powder and baking soda. Add to dates, mixing thoroughly. Stir in well-beaten egg, vanilla and nuts.

Pour into greased and floured 9×5×3-inch loaf pan. Bake in 350°F oven about 1 hour or until toothpick inserted in center comes out clean. Cool in pan, set on rack, 20 minutes.

Remove loaf from pan, set on rack, top side up. When cold, wrap and store overnight before slicing.

TIP

An easy, hand-mixed quick bread. The moist, fruity slices help to make delicious cream cheese sandwiches.

MIXED FRUIT COMPOTE

MAKES 6 SERVINGS

1 cup *Coca-Cola®*

1 cup water

¾ cup orange juice

½ teaspoon almond extract

1 can (21 ounces) cherry pie filling

1 can (16 ounces) sliced peaches, drained

1 cup dried cranberries

Fresh mint leaves (optional)

Combine *Coca-Cola*, water, orange juice and almond extract in large saucepan; mix well. Add pie filling, peaches and cranberries to *Coca-Cola* mixture.

Bring fruit mixture to a boil over medium-high heat. Reduce temperature to low and simmer 12 to 15 minutes or until fruit is tender. Serve warm, at room temperature or chilled. Garnish with mint leaves, if desired.

DESSERTS & BEVERAGES

GINGERBREAD DELUXE

MAKES 4 TO 6 SERVINGS

1 package (14 ounces)
    gingerbread mix

1 tablespoon instant coffee

1 tablespoon grated orange
    peel

¼ cup orange juice

¾ cup *Coca-Cola*®

Combine all ingredients. Beat vigorously with spoon about 1½ minutes or until very well blended.

Pour into 8×8×2-inch greased and floured pan. Bake in 350°F oven 30 to 35 minutes or until center springs back when lightly touched.

Cool 10 minutes; remove from pan and set on rack. Serve as a hot bread or as a dessert with whipped topping.

CHOCOLATE COCA-COLA® CAKE WITH CHOCOLATE CREAM CHEESE FROSTING

MAKES 1 CAKE

1 box (18¼ ounces) chocolate cake mix

1 cup *Coca-Cola*®

¼ cup water

½ cup oil

3 eggs

Chocolate Cream Cheese Frosting (recipe follows)

CHOCOLATE CREAM CHEESE FROSTING

4 cups powdered sugar, sifted

⅓ cup unsweetened cocoa powder

1 package (8 ounces) cream cheese, softened

½ cup (1 stick) butter, softened

1 teaspoon vanilla

Preheat oven to 350°F. Grease two 8-inch round cake pans; set aside.

Combine cake mix, *Coca-Cola*, water, oil and eggs in large bowl. Beat at low speed of electric mixer until blended; beat at medium speed 2 minutes. Divide batter between prepared pans.

Bake 30 to 35 minutes or until toothpick inserted into center of cakes comes out clean. Cool in pans on wire racks 10 minutes. Remove from pans to wire racks; cool completely.

Meanwhile, prepare Chocolate Cream Cheese Frosting. Combine sifted powdered sugar and cocoa in large bowl; set aside.

Beat cream cheese, butter and vanilla extract in large bowl until smooth. Gradually fold in powdered sugar and cocoa.

Place 1 cake layer on serving plate and frost top and sides with Chocolate Cream Cheese Frosting. Repeat with second layer.

DESSERTS & BEVERAGES

COCA-COLA® CHERRY SALAD

MAKES 8 SERVINGS

1 can (21 ounces) cherry pie filling

½ cup water

1 package (4-serving size) cherry gelatin mix

1 can (7½ ounces) crushed pineapple, undrained

1 can (12 ounces) *Coca-Cola*®

½ cup chopped nuts

1 container (8 ounces) chilled whipped topping

1 package (3 ounces) cream cheese

Bring pie filling and water to a boil in medium saucepan over high heat. Remove from heat; add gelatin mix. Stir until mixed.

Add pineapple and juice. Add *Coca-Cola*; stir to combine.

Stir in nuts; refrigerate until set.

Meanwhile, mix together whipped topping and cream cheese. Spread or dollop over cooled and set salad. Serve.

MOLTEN LAVA COCA-COLA® CAKES

MAKES 5 CAKES

5 ounces 60% bittersweet
chocolate, chopped

1 tablespoon butter

4 tablespoons heavy cream

2 eggs plus 1 egg yolk

2 tablespoons *Coca-Cola*®

¼ cup oil

1 package (about 10 ounces)
brownie mix

Powdered sugar (optional)

Whipped cream (optional)

Preheat oven to 400°F. Melt chocolate and butter in small saucepan over low heat; remove from heat and stir in heavy cream.

Beat 2 eggs and 1 egg yolk in small bowl 1 minute until frothy. Add *Coca-Cola* and oil. Beat in brownie mix and melted chocolate mixture.

Place five 3-ounce greased ramekins on baking sheet. Pour about 1 cup batter into ramekins; bake 14 to 16 minutes or until outside edges are set. Cool 3 to 4 minutes.

To serve, loosen edges of cake from ramekins by using a knife along edges to invert onto plate. Top with powdered sugar and whipped cream, if desired.

TIP

No one will be able to resist these tempting
cakes with their melted sweet fillings.

DESSERTS & BEVERAGES

COCA-COLA® CARROT CUPCAKES

MAKES 12 CUPCAKES

3 eggs

½ cup plus 2 tablespoons oil

¼ cup plus 2 tablespoons *Coca-Cola®*

½ cup granulated sugar

¼ cup packed brown sugar

1½ cups all-purpose flour

1 teaspoon baking soda

1 teaspoon baking powder

1 teaspoon ground cinnamon

½ teaspoon ground cloves

½ teaspoon ground nutmeg

½ teaspoon salt

½ teaspoon ground ginger

¾ cup grated carrots

Cream Cheese Icing (recipe follows)

Preheat oven to 350°F. Combine eggs, oil, *Coca-Cola*, granulated sugar and brown sugar in large mixing bowl; blend until smooth.

Add all dry ingredients to bowl; stir until well combined.

Stir in carrots and mix to combine. Pour about ¼ cup batter into 12 paper-lined or greased muffin cups. Bake 15 minutes or until knife inserted into center of cupcakes comes out clean.

Cool completely; frost with Cream Cheese Icing.

CREAM CHEESE ICING

1 package cream cheese or Neufchâtel, softened

1¼ cups powdered sugar

1 tablespoon milk, or as needed

Beat cream cheese and powdered sugar until light and creamy; add milk as needed to adjust consistency.

DESSERTS & BEVERAGES

FUDGEY COCA-COLA® BROWNIES

MAKES 16 SERVINGS

4 unsweetened chocolate baking squares (1 ounce each)

½ cup (1 stick) butter or margarine

1 cup granulated sugar

¾ cup firmly packed dark brown sugar

2 eggs

2 tablespoons *Coca-Cola®*

1 cup all-purpose flour

1 teaspoon vanilla

Coca-Cola® Frosting (recipe follows)

Preheat oven to 350°F. Line bottom and sides of 8-inch pan with foil; lightly grease foil.

Microwave chocolate squares and butter in a large microwave-safe bowl at HIGH 1½ to 2 minutes or until melted and smooth, stirring at 30-second intervals. Whisk in granulated and brown sugars. Add eggs, 1 at a time, whisking just until blended after each addition. Whisk in *Coca-Cola*, flour and vanilla. Pour mixture into prepared pan.

Bake 40 to 45 minutes or until toothpick inserted into center comes out clean. Cool completely on wire rack and cut brownies into 16 squares. Top with *Coca-Cola* Frosting.

COCA-COLA® FROSTING

¼ cup (½ stick) butter or margarine

3 tablespoons *Coca-Cola®*

2 tablespoons cocoa powder

1⅓ cups powdered sugar, sifted

½ teaspoon vanilla

Heat butter, *Coca-Cola* and cocoa in medium saucepan over medium-low heat, stirring until butter melts. Remove from heat and whisk in sugar and vanilla. Set aside.

DESSERTS & BEVERAGES

MOCHA COCA-COLA® FLOAT

MAKES 4 SERVINGS

1 cup coffee ice cream

1 cup vanilla ice cream

2 cups *Coca-Cola®*

1 cup whipped cream

4 teaspoons mini chocolate chips

Scoop ¼ cup coffee ice cream and ¼ cup vanilla ice cream into 4 tall, chilled glasses. Slowly pour in ½ cup *Coca-Cola* into each glass. Top each evenly with whipped cream and chocolate chips. Serve with straw and long spoon.

NOTE

Does it matter if you add the ice cream or the soda first? Adding the ice cream first prevents splashing and overflowing!

COCA-COLA® PECAN PIE

MAKES 8 TO 10 SERVINGS

1 package (15 ounces) refrigerated pie crust

3 eggs

¾ cup sugar

½ cup corn syrup

¼ cup *Coca-Cola®*

2 tablespoons butter or margarine, melted

1½ teaspoons vanilla

¼ teaspoon salt

1½ cups pecan halves

Vanilla ice cream (optional)

Preheat oven to 350°F. Unroll 1 pie crust and place in 9-inch pie plate. Unroll remaining crust and press over bottom crust; gently press crusts together. Fold edges under and crimp.

Combine eggs, sugar, corn syrup, *Coca-Cola*, butter, vanilla and salt in large bowl; stir in pecans. Pour filling into pie crust. Bake 55 minutes or until set. Serve warm or cold with ice cream, if desired.

TIP

Your kitchen will be filled with heavenly aromas when you make this family-favorite classic pie.

DESSERTS & BEVERAGES

INDEX

INDEX

INDEX

METRIC CONVERSION CHART

VOLUME MEASUREMENTS (dry)

$\frac{1}{8}$ teaspoon = 0.5 mL
$\frac{1}{4}$ teaspoon = 1 mL
$\frac{1}{2}$ teaspoon = 2 mL
$\frac{3}{4}$ teaspoon = 4 mL
1 teaspoon = 5 mL
1 tablespoon = 15 mL
2 tablespoons = 30 mL
$\frac{1}{4}$ cup = 60 mL
$\frac{1}{3}$ cup = 75 mL
$\frac{1}{2}$ cup = 125 mL
$\frac{2}{3}$ cup = 150 mL
$\frac{3}{4}$ cup = 175 mL
1 cup = 250 mL
2 cups = 1 pint = 500 mL
3 cups = 750 mL
4 cups = 1 quart = 1 L

VOLUME MEASUREMENTS (fluid)

1 fluid ounce (2 tablespoons) = 30 mL
4 fluid ounces ($\frac{1}{2}$ cup) = 125 mL
8 fluid ounces (1 cup) = 250 mL
12 fluid ounces ($1\frac{1}{2}$ cups) = 375 mL
16 fluid ounces (2 cups) = 500 mL

WEIGHTS (mass)

$\frac{1}{2}$ ounce = 15 g
1 ounce = 30 g
3 ounces = 90 g
4 ounces = 120 g
8 ounces = 225 g
10 ounces = 285 g
12 ounces = 360 g
16 ounces = 1 pound = 450 g

DIMENSIONS

$\frac{1}{16}$ inch = 2 mm
$\frac{1}{8}$ inch = 3 mm
$\frac{1}{4}$ inch = 6 mm
$\frac{1}{2}$ inch = 1.5 cm
$\frac{3}{4}$ inch = 2 cm
1 inch = 2.5 cm

OVEN TEMPERATURES

250°F = 120°C
275°F = 140°C
300°F = 150°C
325°F = 160°C
350°F = 180°C
375°F = 190°C
400°F = 200°C
425°F = 220°C
450°F = 230°C

BAKING PAN SIZES

Utensil	Size in Inches/Quarts	Metric Volume	Size in Centimeters
Baking or	8×8×2	2 L	20×20×5
Cake Pan	9×9×2	2.5 L	23×23×5
(square or	12×8×2	3 L	30×20×5
rectangular)	13×9×2	3.5 L	33×23×5
Loaf Pan	8×4×3	1.5 L	20×10×7
	9×5×3	2 L	23×13×7
Round Layer	8×1½	1.2 L	20×4
Cake Pan	9×1½	1.5 L	23×4
Pie Plate	8×1¼	750 mL	20×3
	9×1¼	1 L	23×3
Baking Dish	1 quart	1 L	—
or Casserole	1½ quart	1.5 L	—
	2 quart	2 L	—